INSPIRATION CORNER

INSPIRATION CORNER

How to Induce the Right Inspiration that

Transforms your Life from the Inside Out

ANTHONY L. WILLIAMS

"Change your mind, change your future"

Anthony Williams/Publisher/2016

First published in 2016 by Anthony Williams
New Bern, North Carolina 28562

Library of Congress Control Number: 2016901201

Notes from the author: The information and personal stories given
in this work are all recollections of a true science and events. The
science presented herein works; however, if you need physical or
psychological help please see a licensed practitioner. I am not a
physician nor am I here to give psychological diagnostics or
remedies. But, I am here to reveal a true path to personal
transformation.

ISBN: 978-0-692-62235-3

Cover design and illustrations by Pixel Studio
Edited by Dr. Ann-Marie Y. Anthony-Williams
Eye of Ra (Re) on interior by Argentium Outlaw
Interior design and typesetting by Anthony L. Williams

ISBN: 978-0-692-62235-3 (softcover)
ISBN: 0-692-62235-7 (softcover)

Dedication

I dedicate this work to my children Bernadette N. Williams, Bernadine S. Williams, Anthony B. Williams, and Gizelle K. M. Roland-Jones. I hope you find the guidance herein to lighten your journey, and to the sleeping giant within, I command you to rise like Lazarus.

Acknowledgements

I am acknowledging those who were instrumental in helping to bring this thought child to fruition. I think it is of importance that we give thanks to the helping forces that aid us in bringing into being that which was and is for our betterment. The development of this thoughtful and inspiring work is a wonderful gift.

I am giving thanks to the inspired thoughts and imagination that opened up to me, and all those upon whose shoulders I was able to stand. I thank everyone who invested in this work directly and indirectly, knowingly or unknowingly. It is because of all our thoughts and imaginations that this mental child was able to manifest through me, and now help many.

Dr. Ann-Marie Y. Anthony-Williams, thank you for the editing of these inspirations, thoughts, and imagination on paper; and, for being a great friend and partner in life. I also give thanks to a wonderful man whom I would only refer to here as a master teacher. Since he, as my personal messenger, has helped to open my mind as a star-gate; I have never looked back. I always knew there was more to our story here on spaceship earth and now I walk in truth. I am now the messenger: We are all Gods and children of the source. As well, I am grateful to my grandparents who played a major part in guiding my spiritual development as a child. Thanks to all in all.

Inspired Thoughts

Introduction

Having the right mindset is essential to living a fully engaged and fruitful life. The successful man or woman knows that in order to reach a pre-determined goal the correct self-talk is needed. The correct self-talk maintains the right mindset. If the goal seeker is not in tune with his or her goal it will be almost impossible to achieve it, being successful. But, what exactly is success? The author feels that before we move forward, we should over-stand the essence of success. Success is the progressive realization of any worthwhile goal. If a woman or man sets out to be a professor and has realized that achievement, he or she has obtained success. The same holds true for whatever a person's goal is that's been achieved.

Now, success is usually the result of an initial inspiration to do a thing; for example, writing this book. The original meaning of inspiration is derived from the Latin form of inspire, or inspirare. Inspirare, according to the etymology dictionary, means to breathe. Now, breathe is spiritus in Latin and means breath of [a divine force] and it is equal to inspiration. So, your inspired thoughts are given to you from the source, and if acted upon will bring you everything you want.

Still, the seeker of success needs to intake positive material in the form of videos, audios, and books to maintain the correct self-talk because the mind can only output initially what is inputted into it. Here the mind is likened unto a water pump. To pump water from the ocean, first the pump must be primed. However, once the water starts to flow a whole lot more comes out than was used to prime the pump. The pump can now pump water from the ocean. Let us prime our pumps.

This book is intended for anyone who seeks the mechanics of inspiration, whether accomplished or a novice because some people are successful and have no idea of the underlying reasons. For these reasons some loose what they have. To be successful you must stay in the spirit.

The Struggle

Many are frustrated because they have read many self-help books and can't seem to have a breakthrough. If this is you, be happy to know that it is not really your fault! The problem is with your paradigm; once this is addressed, you will start having breakthroughs. However, these breakthroughs may seem small at first. Still, pay attention and stay on the path and soon you will find yourself in a different place mentally. This paradigm shift will help lift you to a higher state mentally and, then later, physically.

Most people fail at trying to accomplish a thing because they don't stick with it long enough to see real change or progress. And, as the aforementioned sentence suggests, they try instead of just doing it. We must be persistent and consistent in our determination to succeed. Only by so doing and applying the principles in this book can you succeed.

Thus, we will have to establish a new point of reference; sort of like a time and date stamp on our subconscious mind. With this new starting point, we must establish new mental pictures for the imagination and quotes for our self-talk. This will help shape our new thoughts. Thoughts are things, and thoughts precede action. Therefore, we can say that thoughts acted upon are causes set into action. So, all we would have to do is figure out the effect that we want and manage our thoughts. Let the journey begin.

Inspiration 1

Unconscious Incompetence

"Take inventory of your life today. If your future self will not thank you for taking the steps that you are presently taking, stop in your tracks. It's time to rethink your path"

If it is true that the beliefs we hold about ourselves are the ones that shape our lives the most, and it is, then, equally true that when we expand our views about ourselves it will expand our lives. We owe it to ourselves to live the best life possible. So, how do we see ourselves is the question; are our views about ourselves empowering or disempowering us? Every few months we should take a good look at our lives. Take inventory of where we are in relation to our goals. Then, we should set a different mental sail to navigate the storms of life. It is said that every cell in the human body is replaced every 11 months. Thus, every 11 months we, physically, become totally new beings. Here it makes perfect sense to expand our consciousness also since nothing stays the same. So, expand or regress; the choice is ours.

An answer is found by examining our conscious mind. Many of us are living in a state of mental incompetence. I am talking in the context of how to really attain our goals; what it takes to realize *that* success. The truth hurts, so don't read this book if you don't want to hear it (the truth). Just go ahead and ask yourself what is it that you really want out of life; what is your life's goal? Then ask yourself how are you going to get it, and what is the plan? I am betting that most people reading this book don't even have the slightest idea what it is that they want out of life. Most people never even thought to ask themselves that question. Therefore, they never saw fit to ask how or more importantly why.

"If you want to walk, you must first think about it. If you want to control your life, you must first control your thinking"

Don't let your mind be like a wild horse, control it, or it will destroy you. Would you use a computer that was programmed in the 80s to do an important task today?

Of course, you would not! But that is similar to what we do when we are not consciously learning new concepts. Our brains are the most complex computers known to man. We must learn to program our computers for success with the right software. If we don't consciously decide what and how we will think, it will be decided for us. What will happen is that we will unconsciously pick up some negative habits (programming) that will destroy our lives. This is why it is so important to take the time and consciously reprogram our conscious minds for success.

Nonetheless, this is why the aforementioned questions are so important to ask oneself. These questions put things in perspective as far as our thinking is concerned; they allow us to uncover our unconscious incompetence. Once we have arrived at this destination, we are really at the starting point of positive personal change. The journey has indeed begun. We must know where we came from, and know where we are to control where we are heading.

So now we know that we don't know what we want to do with our lives. It's time to sit down and do some soul searching. Decide where we want to be in five years. Write down our life's goal and how we plan on achieving this goal. Don't be concerned that it may change because it just might. And, we will discuss that in a later chapter, but for now let's run with what we have written down. Know that life is full of surprises. Today is the present, so receive and unwrap it.

Conscious Competence

"Before we can hold anything physically, we must clearly hold it mentally"

Okay, so to recap from chapter one. We went from unconscious incompetence, not knowing that we didn't know to conscious incompetence, which is now knowing that we don't know. This is a great place to be because now we are awakened to our personal situation. Thus, we now can decide what we want. You will find that I repeat things sometimes as I sincerely think that repetition is the mother of skill.

Let me ask you this question. Let's say you wanted to take a vacation and enjoy life some at a nice resort location. Would you get on a plane if you did not know its destination? No? You are not alone, most rational people would not.

But why not? If I may be so bold let me answer that for you, it's because you never know where we might end up. Well, isn't that the same thing we are doing when we get on the plane of life without a predetermined destination? We could end up anywhere in life, and some of us do. We wake up one morning and ask, "How did I end up here?" Well, I think it was Benjamin Franklin who said it best, and I am paraphrasing here: if we fail to plan we plan on failing.

I think you are starting to get the picture and it is very important that you do. I need you to create a visual of these conversations. You see, images are very important; they help you imagine your possibilities. Have you ever noticed the strange and funny commercials that are on Television? Why do you think these corporations spend millions of dollars on these commercials? The stranger or funnier the commercials the more you will remember it the next time you are in the store. That is one way to get you to spend your money on what they would like you to spend it on.

We can use that same technique to reprogram our minds and change our lives. Let me ask you another question. If you had a young child of your own, would you give him or her some directions, or would you just let him or her run wild and learn on his or her own? The logical answer and yours I hope, is yes. We would guide our young child and give him or her some directions. Now, again, why would we do that? So that our child doesn't pick up bad habits, get out of control and ruin his or her life. Now think about that for a moment and then consider this. Your mind is like a child and your mind gives birth to ideas all the time. If we don't nurture this child into development it will remain infantile, then we will have an underdeveloped child giving birth to premature babies. These underdeveloped children will destroy our lives by default. We must develop our cognitive abilities in order to deliver a healthy brain child that will serve us well.

We are to develop cognition if we intend on capturing the life that is within reach but seems illusive. Start by applying logical thinking to identify the fallacies in our own thinking. We must be able to distinguish truth from fiction, via true thought and negating the emotions. Here, we will create fertile soil for right thinking and inspirations.

With this right thinking we can now choose the thoughts we want to nourish into fruition. Think on purpose and for a purpose. Know that the conscious mind is the guard dog at the gate to the underworld (subconscious mind). The subconscious mind does not think; it just absorbs information. The subconscious mind does not differentiate one concept from another. If information gets past the guard dog, then it is considered to be important knowledge, which is stored for use in our lives for better or worse.

"Energy flows where the Mind goes so stay on the Positive and, stop feeding the Negative"

Therefore, it is important that we choose to control our thinking. Watch mostly good shows, read great books, and listen to wonderful audios because what goes in will manifest in our lives in some form. Doing so will start to connect the right neurons in the brain and help to put our thinking on the path less traveled. Think of it like building brain muscles. We can now clearly define what it is that we want out of life, and come up with a plan. Our plan will only be as good as our thinking. We must clearly see our goal in the mind's eye. This is what I submit to you as conscious competence. We now know that we know what we want to achieve in life. This knowing is powerful!

When our thoughts are crystal clear on what we want we will start to receive inspired thoughts on it; I did with this book. Something else will happen also; our reticular activating system kicks in and we start to notice things that can help us on our journey. We will also start to identify people who can help us. The funny thing is that these helpful things and/or people may have been in our line-of-sight the whole time. But, in our ignorant state we did not know how to apply them for our betterment. As a matter of fact, we did not even know what we truly wanted. It's best to think of our goal every day, and remember, for the magic to truly take place, we must work our plan.

Learn to concentrate the mind on outcomes only. People who are successful have learned the art of concentration; if we can't concentrate those old habits will be even harder to replace. Consider this: 3,000 gallons of water running in the streets will not really affect us if we had to walk through it. But concentrate, that same 3,000 gallons of water through a fireman's hose nozzle and it will knock us off our feet.

Thoughts are things and all things vibrate at different rates. Like vibrations resonate with each other, and therefore, are attracted to each other. If you were to place a piano across the room from another and strike a key on one, the same key will vibrate on the other piano. Consequently, if we allow our minds to dwell on positive thoughts, it must be the result of our manifested reality and vice versa.

Once we get our minds right and are living in the state of conscious competence, we find that the best inspirations come from within; not from this book or any other. Self-help books, videos, and audios are tools to help get your mind right and point you on your way. As Bruce Lee once so astutely put it, (paraphrasing here) one should not look at the object of direction but look at where it is pointing.

Breakthroughs come when you least expect it. If we are always living in our comfort zones, we may get a breakthrough but I beg-to-differ. It is when the storm of life has knocked us down and washed us up and we are about to drown that lightning strikes us with awareness! In the midst of darkness comes light right after the darkest hour.

Desperation will lead to inspiration and what we have been filling our minds with will determine what's on the other side. This book came out of the depths of darkness to be a guiding light to success. I refer to it as the black light because just like a black light, it allows us to see things that were before unseen.

Unconscious Competence

"Your life is a reflection of you! You can only reflect who you are inside. So, don't blame your wife, don't blame your husband, your parents, or the government. That big mess or wonderful life is all your doing. The sooner you take and accept responsibility the better for you...if you don't like what you see, change it"

By now we should be asking this personal question, "Why is it I never questioned myself about what's my life goal and what exactly would it look like to me? More importantly why do I want it?" In other words, why were we in a state of unconscious incompetence?" It is simple; the fact is that most people exist in a state of hypnosis. This particular hypnosis is of negative reinforcement. Most people are being programed by mass media and trained how to group think. A lot of people look for social proof before they do anything. Therefore, if everyone is doing it (something), watching it, talking about it, or believes in it that's the right thing to do. If the truth is to be told, this is why 5% of the population maintains most of the wealth. You see, the top percentile learned a long time ago that the road least traveled leads to success, any success.

Let's address this question here of why we never questioned ourselves in detail. As stated above, we were in a state of unconscious incompetence and may require social proof before making decisions. This, as I also suggested, is because of mass hypnosis. So, besides reading this book, what will cause us to start questioning? Remember in chapter two we discussed how most breakthroughs come when we least expect it; and that light is born out of darkness? I just had a thought, even most of our oldest religious books declare that light came out of darkness.

Why is this metaphor relevant and how does it apply to our discussion? Because out of desperation comes inspiration; remember? And, desperation equals pain, more than likely emotional pain! This pain broke our hypnosis and allowed us to focus on a different reality; our personal reality that's not filled with what kind of car the Jones' have, not what's happening on General Hospital, and not the latest movie in the theater! The only show we are focused on *right now* is called my world, it's flipping upside down and we have to get it back going in the right direction. The right pain will wake us up! It will either make us fold and cower or unfold into a beautiful flower. Once an intelligent person realizes that his or her level of thinking is bringing him or her pain, the only recourse is to change one's thinking.

We live our lives mostly on auto-pilot; there is an invisible force keeping us breathing and our hearts beating. We don't think about how to walk, we don't think about how to drive a vehicle, and we don't think about how to accomplish our everyday task. Now, when we were first learning these tasks we had to think about them. You may not remember when you first started to walk. But, when we watch a toddler we see that he or she falls a few times before actually taking that first step. After numerous practices we can now walk and don't even think about it. It has become a habit and is now accomplished from a subconscious level. We walk as perfectly as our physical bodies will allow. It can be said that we now have an unconscious competence as related to walking.

If we want to be successful in our pursuit of a life goal, we must apply these insights. Since we are now consciously competent about our goal, we can go ahead and determine what are the causes and conditions necessary to create that outcome. Every day when we concentrate on creating the causes and conditions to provide the proper soil in the form of unconscious competence, our dreams will grow into life.

"Once we become Aware of what we really Internally Possess, we will live our Dreams"

You see our goal of a new life can be realized. It is only now that we can turn this dream into a reality because it now exists within the confines of our minds. This particular reality could not have been manifested before because it did not exist before. Let me ask you another question, "How do you think a skyscraper or mansion is created or even a high tech government spy plane?" All of these things must first be imagined. They all must first be created in the mind. Lots of thoughts went into any successful manifestation. There is nothing created on this earth that was not first a thought; even to make breakfast we have to first picture what will be made.

The mind is the creator of everything we seek and imagination its workshop; if trained in the right way it will serve us well. When the right information is presented to and accepted by the conscious mind, it will impregnate the subconscious mind. Planting the right seeds will yield the correct harvest. When the information is accepted as true and their resulting actions carried out on auto-pilot, this is true unconscious competence in action. Repetition is truly the mother of skill.

One's computer is no longer running on outdated software but is now updated to perform the task at hand. Once the mind is tuned to keep it optimized, regular conditioning is needed. Regular intake of positive material relative to one's goal is a must. Old habits sometimes die hard, and if we fail to maintain our new state, regression will set in. After all, there are a lot of social proofs as to why we should do that which will not serve us well. Remember, the mind can be our best ally or our worst enemy. Be the master to the child and it will obey.

Inspiration 4

The Journey

"Life is not going to give you what you want; life is not going to give you what you need; life will only give you what you fight for"

Repetition is the mother of skill. Remember that cause and effect are as important mentally as they are physically! Cognitive causes will have cognitive effects in the subliminal sense that will ultimately affect our physical world. Therefore, our mental and physical realities are inseparable. Our outer world is but a reflection of our inner domain. Still, the power to manifest positive circumstances is ours, if we so choose to use it.

I like stories. As a child growing up in Trinidad, we (the natives of that land) heard many stories that pertained to life that gives us a better over-standing. My wife inspired me to use stories to help us grasp a fuller over-standing of this concept that is shared. She (my wife) doesn't even know of this inspiration. It came after I got wind that her dissertation is about storytelling.

There was once a man who lived up in a mountain for many years. Living as a recluse, one day he had an inspired thought to invent something to be of good use for humanity. Thus, the inventor moved down the mountain closer to civilization because he knew he would need the use of electricity, a new discovery. While working in his cabin, he started plugging in all sorts of gargets for experimentation. Unfortunately, every time he started to make some progress the fuses in the cabin would blow out.

The inventor ended up frustrated and gave up on his work. He declared that electricity was useless and not enough power can be generated for his invention to work. Nonetheless, he decided to stay at his present location and live out the rest of his days. One day a stranger happened by and asked if he may have a glass of water. The resident owner brought out the glass of water to the stranger. As they both sat on the porch talking, the inventor started to tell his story. At the end the inventor stated, "If it wasn't for the fact that electricity was limited my invention would have served many well."

Then, the stranger replied, "I am an electrician and I am here to tell you electricity is not limited. In fact, it is very powerful! The problems are with your wiring and fuses. You, my old friend, need higher gage wires and fuse amperages to accommodate what you are trying to accomplish. I knew the old man who lived here before, all he had was an old radio. Each house is allowed only a certain amount of electrical power to protect its owner from being destroyed. If you don't know what you are doing you could burn down the whole house. Long story short, they both teamed up and brought the invention to the market where many prosper from it.

The moral of the story is that we all have a power within us whose greatness is yet to be quantified; it is the reason for every great creation on this earth. Yet, most of us are unaware of its existence. To use it creatively all we need do is to rewire the way we think. This, in turn, will rewire the neurons in our brain. But, misuse it and it will destroy our world.

I have succeeded at many things in my life, but what is more important is that I have also failed. Failing was good because it is in the failing that we learn and discover the new insights to succeed later. However, most people do not like to fail. Consequently, a lot of people never really reach their goals in life because they are afraid of failing. Fear is our greatest enemy! It is not our fault; yet, we are trained from young that failing is bad. Still, I am here to tell you that we can't learn unless we fail or learn from someone else's mistakes. Think about it, it is only after many hours, days, months, and even years of training does one succeed. It's about mind-set! The key is to take massive action so we can fail faster. You heard me right! Fail as fast as you can. Thus, we will succeed faster. We MUST fail in order to learn. When we were babies we had to fall a few times before we could walk. We had to fall a few more times before we could run. If people fell and stayed down, they would not have learned to walk, much less run. Remember though, the goal is not to keep failing but to succeed as fast as possible.

Why is it that so many people just crawl through life as adults? Life knocked them down and they stayed down. Somewhere along the way we lost our tenacity to grow! We were born to win!!! Life's struggles were meant to make us stronger, not to break our spirits. The best knowledge is the knowledge of self. Seek out the riddle of the caterpillar, and fly like a butterfly. Knowledge is only power when put to use; for, it is not in the knowing but in the doing.

As situations change, plans may have to be adjusted to suit. A plane in flight has to be corrected numerous times to adjust for winds and magnetic variances to reach its destination. It is the same with us; sometimes we will have to adjust our plans or change it altogether. At this point, it is good to know that success is not a destination, it is a progressive journey. When we acquire our goals it will be the breaking of the ice, so to speak, and we will then see bigger and brighter goals to surmount. Our sights will keep getting better.

Imagine looking at the sun setting in the hills; it is a beautiful sight to behold. This same way, you can set out to explore. You will have to go around trees and other obstacles to get there. Upon finding the spot where you saw the sunset in the hills you can now see even further than before. This will inspire you to go even further, and the further you go you will realize that it is a never ending journey. And, each place seems to be much better than the last. The things you have seen along the way, and the people you have meet will change your mindset forever. Now you can never go back, your life is changed forever. It's about who you become on your journey.

Stay in the Now

"Stop being a spectator all through life; you have got to be in it to win it, this game called life!"

Just like in the movie The Matrix, once a mind is freed it can never go back unless its memory is taken away. If we are enslaved and don't know it, we will remain a slave forever. But, once we are shown what real freedom is we will fight to the death to remain free.

Nonetheless, in this game called life we have to know how to play. What are the rules and are there consequences. John F. Kennedy once said, "Ask not what the country can do for you, but what can you do for the country." In my opinion, John F. Kennedy was very wise in his assessment of how to use one's energies. We call upon a certain power when we seek to serve many and that is exactly what he was saying, ask not what the people can do for us, but find out how we can serve the people. When we find a way to serve many, then success will be within our grasp.

I think there is something called the law of one and what we do must be in accordance with this law. Let me explain. Remember when I said that thoughts are things; well, what exactly is a thought? Thought is energy. Individually, we are and are not the originators of this energy. No, I am not trying to confuse you. It is an oxymoron. This energy has a source; let's call it the Mental Ocean. We are a part of this energy and just like the molecules in our bodies are individual and separate, they all, each and every one, has our whole DNA within them. It follows that we as part of this source are, thus, in fact the source. But, the real power comes from the source itself in which we are connected as one. With this rationalization and realization know that we all are one.

As a consequence, if what we do does not support the one which is all, we will not be successful for long. Consider this, if you fill a glass of water from the ocean, then fill a teacup, and next a mug of water from the ocean, is the water inside different or the same in each? When the water in all evaporates, will it not go back to the source from whence it came? What makes you think you are different from me, or even the source? We are but one. The truth rests inside us and in there you will find me. Yet, a glass must be a glass, and a teacup a teacup as a mug remains a mug. It can be said that the source expresses itself in multiple ways. Realize that we are in all and all is in us, and what we send out will return to us.

Knowing this we should not hold any negative thoughts one for another as this will be counterproductive. Anger, unfairness, jealousy, or any kind of negative emotion toward oneself or another will impede us. The energies that we are working with are inclined to love and care! Just look around today at all the big companies and countries that are now falling apart. It is their greed, not in acquiring wealth but in what they did with it, and by what means. Wealth and abundance are good and every knowing body that is connected to source consciously should and would grow in abundance. Source is abundance and we can't help anyone if we can't help ourselves. But, selfishness is a negative energy that will destroy any unworthy cause built on it. Let this be our example, we breathe out carbon dioxide, which in turn supports the trees through photosynthesis. The trees in turn emit oxygen and this supports our physical life on this planet. This is how life works; all we have to do is look to nature and observe natural law.

It is important to stay present; live in the now. What is happening in the now is the only reality. This is it! The past is no longer, it only lives on in our memories. The future is nonexistent as it depends on us to create it. The future has many possibilities in which direction it could go. The only reality is now, this moment here with me. The decisions we make in the now will determine our future; for, it will create it. And, as we change our minds, our future changes with it. So, stay in the now and enjoy it to the fullest.

Inspiration 6

Reality

"The conscious mind through imagination, molded in feeling, is your reality"

What is reality and is reality really real? When we look at a thing long enough, the way we look at it changes. When the way we look at a thing changes, the thing we look at changes. Hence, the way we view things will determine the reality we live in. Is your glass half empty or half full? Based on our points of reference we will see the same things differently. Thus, two people living in the same world will experience totally different realities.

If we live in abundance, we have a time reference of abundance. Therefore, our glass will be half full as we work with the law of increase. Yet, those who have a time reference of lack will see the glass as half empty; they are working with the law of decrease. This is why we must learn to alter our points of reference. Learn to always work with the law of increase and abundance. Don't let your demographics determine your destiny. If you physically live in an undesirable place, find a mental alternate. Consciously chose your path to success. Be in the world, but not of that world, and soon you will extricate yourself from it.

You must be willing to leave it all behind you until you so develop your mind to handle it. Stop holding on to the baggage that's keeping you in someone else's bag! Let go and let life manifest from within you. If you refuse to let go of past baggage, you are holding yourself back. Your outer persona can only reflect what's inside. The lesson is repeated until it is learned; hopefully in this life.

In the next few years, you will become the average of the five people you hang around the most. What this means to you is that you have some hard choices to make. Am I saying to get rid of your no-good-friends? No, I can't tell you what to do (all I can say is that is exactly what I did!). However, if you want to make some positive changes in your life, and make the next five years better than the last five; you should change your thinking. This ultimately leads to a change of one's environment, even if it's mentally initially. The choice is ours. Change your mindset, change your future.

Reality is nothing but a mental projection on the screen of life: the images, beliefs, and convictions we hold in the subconscious mind. It could be said that we live in a hologram of life that we have created for ourselves. This creation can be consciously or unconsciously created.

Henceforth, it will do us good to remember that if we want to change our reality, we must change the programming that was passed on to the subconscious. Repetition is the mother of skill and by now you should have an over-standing of this knowledge. It has been stated in many different ways. No longer should you be standing under this knowledge in ignorance of application. If in fact this is for you, then you should be standing over it as the master ready to command. If not now, when? Now is the only real existence.

Self-Empowerment

"You are the Potter Sitting at the Wheel of Imagination"

Take action now! I don't care how small or great this action is, it's important that you do it and do it now. A body at rest stays at rest, but a body in motion picks up momentum. It is the same with the mind; we must put the mind into action right away and the action of the mind is thought. As we have mentioned before the only constant is change; either our minds are getting stronger or weaker. Nothing stays the same.

Have you ever wondered why we patent a new invention which, by the way, is a new thought? When we get an inspiration from source, we must take fast and massive action. If we don't take action, the source of that inspired thought will find someone else who will. So, we use patents to say a particular thought was given to us first.

All inspired thoughts come from the source of all things. The All in All is the source also referred to as God, the Universal Mind, Devine Intelligence, and a lot of other names in different languages and cultures around the world. Nonetheless, when we are in tune with this force, we will receive inspirational thoughts. Many have tapped into this force by accident. But, when we learn to vibrate on the same frequency as source, we become the captain of our own ship!

Earlier we stated that if one piano is placed across the room from another and a note is struck, the same will vibrate on the other instrument. What we did not say is this remains true if both are tuned correctly. This means they must be in tune with each other. Therefore, the second piano's note must be sympathetic with the source note. In this same way, we must raise our vibrational levels to resonate with source, and realize that interdependency. We must become a creative instrument of the creative force and be as creators. For this to happen, action must be taken to facilitate skillful thoughts and we must build new connections. We are talking about neurons bridging each other in new form; new wiring for new power. Then, the right physical action will follow to help us on our journey.

Remember that the best things in life are thoughts. Even so, thoughts without action is like a miscarriage of one's brain child just the same way action without thoughts is like unto hunting in the dark. Your personal power is in taking action about a worthy idea; and the more action the better. To grow oak trees, three times the amount needed must be planted as seeds. To impregnate a female's egg, over 7,000,000 sperms are lunched and only one survives. That one was you, so be happy and productive. Nature always shows us what we should be doing, but are we listening? Take massive action and empower yourself today.

Everything is in motion in this universe. Consider the solar system and how all objects rotate around the sun, and this includes our home. Even here, at home, the movement of the ocean is a constant thing. Life is in continuous motion. Likewise, our bodies must also stay in motion to remain in optimal condition. To remain healthy, we must partake in regular exercise. Physical exercise helps to keep our bones, tendons, and muscles strong. As well, exercise is good for our cardiovascular and circulatory systems. Here the circulatory system is evidence that even within our bodies there is motion. The more we exercise the stronger we get.

It is the same with our cognition. We must keep our cognitive health in proper condition. Many people exercise their bodies but fail to exercise their cognitive abilities. Here we need the whole package to gain total personal empowerment. The more personal power we generate, the better chance of accomplishing our mission. However, special attention must be paid to our cognitive awareness and concentration. You may need a degree of moral courage to do what's right for you. But once you take action you will have harness the power.

Inspiration 8

Possibilities

"Leaders have Vision; they look into the Future and see Possibilities. Leaders don't focus on the Problem; they focus on the Solution"

Note that in order to control the events in our lives, we must first control the causes which are thoughts. That is the solution to a better future; by focusing on our now we build the future. Once we over-stand that we could tap into the mental ocean, a realization sets in that all is possible. We become as architectures and start designing our realities with constructive thoughts. A key has been given and when the student is ready the master waits behind the door. By using right thinking, concentration, and visualization we can raise our vibrations. Open your mind, it is the doorway to the temple of wisdom.

Going forward keep the self-talk positive, don't concentrate on what we don't want but on what we do want. We must stay in tune with the higher vibrations and use the law of growth. This is one of the purposes of life; look around us at nature, everything is either growing or dying. Are we satisfied with the reality we have manifested thus far? We must learn to grow our mental faculties or they will dissipate.

It is time for us to rise like a phoenix out of the ashes of our old lives into the new. As I become aware of this power in me, there is a responsibility to inform those asleep. Then, maybe we can protect our home for the betterment of all. The possibilities of a collective reality that can benefit all are enormous. Just look around at what is taking place in the world today. We need a collective positive flow of energy.

There are many people who just sit back and wait for things to change. They pray every day for things to change; for a better life, for a better world. But where there is pray there must be meditation. Pray is the asking and meditation being the listening. When we listen we will find out that the source can't do for us what it can only do through us! Do the work! Let's go ahead and give ourselves permission to think bigger; moreover, take action to become who we were meant to be. Love the persons we are today, but don't let those persons we are today keep us from becoming the people we could be tomorrow.

Possibilities

We should not be content with less than our worth. Use the key! At this very moment the consciousness of possibilities stands waiting at the door. No one can open that door but us. No, not collectively, I am talking about you; you must do it. It is your birthright; you owe it to yourself to be the best possible you. If you are in your darkest hour, now is the time to let in the dawn of a new era of possibilities. Even if it's not the darkest hour, it's time for a positive change, isn't it? Go ahead and step into it.

Hey, let me tell you a little something about possibilities. Colonel Sanders was 65-years old when he franchised his restaurant Kentucky Fried Chicken. It's never too late. Thomas Edison was credited with inventing the modern light bulb; as legend would have it he made 999 tries before he got it right. It takes persistence and consistence. Michael Jordan was benched during the beginning of his basketball career they told him he wasn't good enough. Well, we know how that turned out. Just in case you don't, Michael Jordan became one of the best players of all times. I think we are starting to get the picture. They all used their personal power in its entirety to become overachievers in their lanes. We can do it also, and no one can tell us what we can or can't do but our individual self. If the mind can create something, hold it and believe it, we can achieve it.

Inspiration 9

Checks and Balances

"We could make excuses or we could make progress, but we can't do both in the same time and space"

One could define checks and balances as a principle related to a governing force. Within this principle, separate domains are empowered to control individual actions made by each other. And, each domain is induced to share its power. This is the definition I submit to you as it applies to our governing faculties.

What does control your thoughts mean? I have been on this quest of knowledge for 35 years. I am talking about knowledge on the deeper workings of the mind, and how to apply it for success. I had always run into that saying: to be successful, one must learn to control his or her thoughts. Were these teachers talking about when doing a task, to think about what one was doing? Not quite, although we should concentrate on the task at hand. It was not until I started to tap into my inner power source that things started to take shape. We must control our daily thought-process. I am talking about painstaking monitoring of our thoughts.

Thoughts are things and everything has a vibration. Some thoughts vibrate high and some low. Our goal is to vibrate as high as we can, this will put us in harmony with our higher selves. So, today is July 30th, 2014. Yesterday, during the shadow hours after starting this chapter, I was wondering how it would take form. To be specific, how am I to confer to you the reader a means whereby you can control your thoughts? As I was taking a shower, I thought long and hard about telling you this. Why? Anthony Robbins had an epiphany in a similar manner. I did not want you or him to think, well, I misappropriated a script out of his life. Even so, I am an indirect mentee of Tony Robbins.

Now that I've got that out of the way this is what happened. As I was taking a shower during the shadow hours, the word compartmentalize, just popped into my head. As I kept thinking about the word I suddenly realized, "Yes, we need to compartmentalize our thoughts to an allotted period of time throughout the day." There I am standing in the shower and this inspiration just comes to me. Now, I am wondering if water gives us a stronger connection to source since Tony Robbins had at least one great premise while in the shower as well. But, that is something I will have to research in-depth. At this point, here is the other dilemma I had. While drying myself off I started to think, and wondered, did I just make up that word or not. I knew about the word compartment, but compartmentalize; the more I thought about it consciously, the more it sounded like a made up word. I hurried up, got dressed and sat at the computer to look up this word; and guess what, it is a word. I know some of you who knew this word already maybe saying really? Yes! And, you may be a psychology major. Anyway, I went to bed and today I am seeing if it fits in context with what is being presented. However, now that I am sure it came from source there is no doubt in my mind that it does.

We are to compartmentalize our thoughts. If you have never really done much mind work before, you will find out quickly that the faint need not apply; even though, the weak minded are those who need it the most. Yet, we all need to work on this to manifest our desired reality. I know it seem like this will be a big job and it will take some time, but I promise you the payoff is priceless. Someone once said a mouse can eat an elephant one bite at a time. Let's start by breaking our day into four parts; our conscious part of the day, that is. You will have to apply this to your day as you see fit as we all wake and return to sleep at different hours.

On a regular day I will rise at 7:00AM and be in bed by 12 midnight. That would mean that I am physically awake for a total of 17 hours. Here, we break those 17 hours into 4-

hours and 15-minutes compartments. You could play with this to adjust for what it is you are trying to accomplish. This is just an example: The first four hours and 15 minutes I would decide to consciously think I am one with my higher self. The second quarter I am thinking I am creating more wealth in my life. In the third quarter my thoughts are this is not my final outcome, I am waiting for my outer reality to reflect my inner reality. And, the last quarter I am open to inspiration from the source. Note: in the statement I am creating more wealth in my life wealth to me is health, love, and money.

You don't have to use the words that I use here. Any positive words that vibrate high will do. The main purpose of this exercise is to restrain our thoughts. Be warned, the mind doesn't like to be watched; thus, it will try to trick you. By using a systematic approach to controlling our thoughts, we can now build new connections in our brains. It takes about 30 days to create a new habit; I suggest we do this for at least that period. What we think about the most will be.

Okay, now that we have our thoughts somewhat under control, let's work on those goals we set earlier. We have to see what we want crystal clear in our minds. Those goals are the outcome we want. While I was in the Marine Corps, we used to apply something called reverse planning. Let's use a similar approach here, but adjusted for within this context. Since we know the outcome, we can start there and in our minds trace back step by step how that outcome unfolded. We do this until we find the cause that facilitated the growth of that outcome. If we have been paying attention; then, we know what that is. The only thing left to do is to create the causation that will result in said conditions.

The mind governs the body and our realities. Reality is a perception of thought. The principle of this governing force is simple. Separate levels of the mind are responsible for certain functions. Mind is spiritual power, as no one had seen the mind at any time. Mind is energy and the power of creation. A conscious mind decides what is relevant to our goals then pass it to the subconscious. The subconscious is that part of us in connection with source. Once we decide; make a decision of choice, this power of creation will reflect to us our inner truths. No one is completely so-called negative or positive, but to get what we want there are checks and balances to consider within.

Inspiration 10

Fear

"The only way to get out of the box is to learn to think outside of the box"

What prison/s have we created for ourselves? Sometimes, we create prisons for ourselves and don't even realize that we are the jailers restraining our freedom! Here I give you the biggest reason why many have failed to reach their destiny after clearly defining it; fear. During my experience in the Marine Corps, I learned that courage is facing your adversary even though you were afraid. However, for the purposes of this book you must learn to eliminate fear. Fear is a negatively vibrating emotion that cuts off our flow of energy from source. Fear puts us in a very low vibrational field. What most don't realize is that the thing we fear the most hunts us the most. The thing that hunts us the most becomes a reality that imprisons the hunted.

The reality is if we look at our history that which we fear has been illusionary. It has been an unfounded fear. All the same, this fear held us back from attaining our goals. Fear creates a false reality that will paralyze its victim. This paralysis usually disarms its victim of all personal power. I remember while growing up in Trinidad we would enjoy many fruits. That was one of the many things I missed as a teenager in Brooklyn. If we wanted something to eat, we just went outside to find it. Some children found more to eat than others. I reason, it's like adults now-a-days in life's adventure.

The following is what I mean. In Trinidad we had a variety of fruit trees such as cashews, mangos, plums and many others. Let's say we decided to invade the plum tree and there were limited plums on the ground. As this was usually the case, if a plum was really ripe and a bird picked on it that one may fall. Or, maybe, some got knocked on the ground. But, the best ones are on the tree. Now if we did not have something to pick it with, we would have to climb the tree. And, guess where some of the best fruits are on the tree? Out on a limb; that's right, sometimes we have to go out on a limb to get what we want. If we are too fearful to go out on a limb, we just may not get what we want. Most of us who climbed the tree found out that the fears we had of being up there were unreal. When the pain of being hungry outweighs the pain of what we think the fear will do, we will climb to the top.

Accordingly, fear of the unknown is usually a made up negative reality that keeps many of us immobilized. This fear is usually a product of unguided imagination and has no basis in truth. When we seek out the truth behind and in all things fear must die. Once we know the truth, we can step forward in faith because when we build on facts, we know the circumstance we seek as well as the cause to create it. This is the substance of things we want; the evidence of things yet to be realized. Therefore, fear has no place to strive.

"Sometimes we may feel Boxed in by outside Circumstances, but if we want to live outside the Box, we must first learn to think outside the Box"

When we look at financially successful people and note their stories, we will find that they learn to think differently than the masses. What the herd sees as risks, complexity, or adversity the rich see as opportunity. YOU are not willing to take the risks. This is why five percent of the population controls the money. The 95% seem to not know how to think outside of the box; learn to take a calculated risk and do something new. It is time to break our mass hypnosis.

Consider the following: You are to sculpture a piece of marble. You were given a chisel and hammer and before you are the marble. You have a wonderful image in your head but you are afraid to start chiseling. You think that if you start, the first hit of chisel and hammer will destroy the marble so you just stand there. The person next to you is in the same predicament; still, he or she started and now has an image sculptured out. It's not perfect, but all the same, it has form. Because of the other person's actions he or she has figured out the secret; he or she asks for a smaller chisel and creates a masterpiece. You then ask him or her, what is the secret. He or she replies, the secret is there is no secret; but, know this, if you don't start you can't finish and the marble is your life.

I recall many of my family and friends asking, "Tony, weren't you afraid to go into the Marine Corps?? When I asked what they meant, most of the time they were referring to Marine Corps Boot Camp. There is a certain reputation surrounding Marine Corps Boot Camp. I was always temped to say no, and in a way that would be true. But, the truth is almost everyone on that plane heading to Paris Island was concerned about unknown expectations. All one had to do was look into the eyes of these candidates and note their behavior to tell. First, I was very much afraid. However, when I would sit watching television with my father he would put on war movies; after watching, he would ask me if I still wanted to enlist in the Marines. This made me think deeply about my decision so I mentally reasoned it out. I sought the facts about boot camp and the whole Marine Corps idea. My conclusion was this, if one man can do it so could I. A lot of recruits weren't dying in boot camp. It was either you made it or you did not. I was in top shape physically and mentally, and had determination. Plus, I went in with leverage; I had a daughter on the way and needed to support her. Those were the facts. Thus, there was no room left for fear; I knew the truth. I ended up staying 20 years in the Marine Corps. We have to decide whether we will live our dreams or live our fears. It will be one or the other; the choice is ours.

I will end this chapter with a true account I recalled from business school. I really wish I could remember the exact source it came from but I can't. However, it left a lasting impact on me and I just thought I would share it here. I hope it drives home the moral of this chapter. As I recall, the narrative goes something like this. Now bear in mind this is a rendition of an actual event. A man wondered upon a refrigeration truck and ventured inside. Somehow the doors of the truck closed and the man was trapped inside. The next morning, he was found in the truck frozen to death.

The odd thing was that the truck's freezing system had been broken for some time before this incident. On proper examination of the dead man's body, it was found that he had been frozen to death by fear. You see, even though he was locked inside the freezing compartment, the truck's air output was no more than that required to air-condition a home. This man's fear created a mental condition that froze him to death. Thoughts are things!

Freedom

"We must go through it to get through it. Weather the Storm with a Positive Expectation of Sunshine on the other side"

Once we get past the invisible wall of fear and the other negative thoughts, we free our self from their mental prison. The formerly enslaved now takes his or her rightful place as master. You are the master of your own life for good or bad. The choice is yours. Now the elephant has broken its mental conditioning and knows its true power. As a baby, elephants are tied to a small metal pole that is buried partway in the ground. At that point in their lives they are not strong enough to pull this pole out; thus, they are confined to it. Nonetheless, once these elephants are fully grown that metal pole is replaced with a small wooden stake that is like a twig; in that, if the elephants move, the twig will snap and be unnoticeable to them. But, because they were conditioned as babies, they no longer try to escape. The new prisons are in their heads. Recognize the elephant in the room and know we have the most powerful force at our beck and call waiting on its master. When the master is ready, the servant will appear ready to serve.

Accordingly, let's take life by its horns and ride it to the destiny of our choosing. We must become the Chief Executive Officers of our own affairs. Clearly see the vision, analyze and find the cause to the condition, motivate ourselves, and do the work. We are to run our lives like a business because it is our business. This reinvention of ourselves is a very innovative period in our lives. We now, also, have to take responsibility for our own lives and everything that happens in it. This is real freedom; conscious freedom. But remember, if our thinking is faulty, we will have defective results. It starts with us and ends with us.

This kind of freedom gives us the power to be players in the game; most are merely in the game, literally as pieces, pawn or queen it doesn't matter. The mental masters are the players of the game who controls it. If you are reading this book; then, it was drawn to you or you to it. It's time to master our reality instead of being controlled on the board of life; let's manipulate the whole board.

Some food for thought; sometimes we may have that clear vision of our destiny. However, I know a whole working plan to get there may not be clearly visible at times. Think about this, a man driving in a car in the late hours can only see as far as the headlights will allow. Consequently, we may need to lay the 'road' as we walk towards our goal/s. As was stated before, sometimes we may even have to go out on a limb; yet, a small cost to pay for freedom. I have been a success at many things in my life and each came with a price. You must pay the price. At times you have to go through things (some experiences) to get to your goals. Don't let small hurdles keep you from achieving great things, follow your dreams.

Knowing that our objective mind has impregnated our subconscious mind with the right information, we can now relax. Let our subjective mind guide us to our goal on auto pilot. Hence, knowing this we should be confident that victory is ours. Step out on faith with a positive knowing and expectation even if the uncertainty of not seeing the whole road is there. We know and trust the subjective mind which is connected to the mental reservoir and knows the way. Trust in yourself! You now hold the scepter of consciousness to self-rule.

Build a Relationship

"The Destiny we seek is already here"

How well do we know ourselves? Think about it, when was the last time you spent some time alone. From time to time we need to spend quality time alone. We spend quality time with those we love. The question is, do you love you? Do you even really know the answer to that question? Some will give the kneejerk response by saying, "Of course I do, I love me." But really, how do you know? Unless a person has undergone certain steps to know, he or she doesn't know.

Love emits a very strong positive vibration to bring us what we want; I have used it as such. Love helps us to vibrate in harmony with the mental reservoir but this love must be an honest feeling. I would sit down in a relaxed state and concentrate on divine love. Then I would think of everyone I disliked and surround them in this love. Here, I would really aim to change my feelings about them. But, know this, we can say we love someone; yet, we can't truly love others unless we first love ourselves.

Learn to build a relationship with your higher self. From this point, we can then communicate what we need from source. Just like in an intimate relationship, we can't expect our significant other to know what we want and need unless it is voiced. We have to relate in a relationship for it to work. Now if you pissed off your significant other and then try to communicate your wants, it may fall on deaf ears. This is because you are not in tune with each other in the moment; as well, both of you may be in a very negative state called hate. This is the extreme opposite of love on the polarity pole.

This is the very reason we need to get in touch with our inner being. We also need to make peace with ourselves, forgive ourselves, and come to know our true nature/s. After we know who we are, it is time to make a mental decision to accept ourselves for who we are. We must love what we have found inside; the real us. Once this is done we can now take the steps to change unwanted characteristics. With this created oneness with the whole, we can now communicate our desires and expect to receive. Yes, again, you must do the physical work after the mental.

How can this be? Think on this, we came forth from the ALL into the physical still in the ALL. Everything that is and ever will be is right here in the ALL. All we have to do is see what we want, as it is already here, and it will appear to us. It will become part of our reality even as our faith is it unto us. Everything is right here right now, and what we think is what makes the difference. Know this, whether you see it consciously or unconsciously, you own it. Therefore, we must have a harmonious mental attitude to live a pleasant life.

Inspiration 13

Building Power

"The reality we seek is at that moment seeking us"

Knowledge is potential power waiting to be released into action just like a bullet encased in a shell filled with gunpowder which is full of potential power. But, until the bullet is placed in a gun and fired, it cannot take down a target. That must be the Marine Corps residual in me. Yet, acquired knowledge is the same as that bullet. Knowledge in and of itself is static power, but once we take action it comes into play. If we are unable to concentrate, we can't thoughtfully focus our knowledge. Remember, we must be able to focus our thoughts to apply knowledge like water through a fireman's hose nuzzle. Only then will our knowledge be useful and take effect.

One way of strengthening our mental concentration is by developing our listening skills. The next time you are listening to a friend talk, pay attention to what is going on in your head. For the untrained mind there will be a lot of chatter. You will not really be listening to your friend. What you will be doing is waiting for him or her to finish talking so you can talk. You may even interrupt your friend in order for you to talk. As a matter of fact, you will be constantly trying to think of what you will say as soon as you get the chance. Pay attention; that, my friend, is not listening. We must listen to the speaker as though we are to take a post-test of his or her word contents. We should make eye contact, and then watch his or her expressions and body movement. That is true listening, we must concentrate on every word. This, in turn, will allow us to better increase our mental concentration.

Another great exercise is the reading of great books. When reading try to hold your complete attention on what you are reading. When the mind drifts, just bring it back to concentrate on the content of the book. Try to read a whole chapter without thinking about anything else except for the content. Even if you stop to contemplate a sentence or paragraph, hold the focus. Additionally, you can sit quietly eye closed and for 10 minutes let your mind think only of your breathing and your heart beat. Whatever you find yourself doing, make a game of it. See how long you can hold your attention on a subject to the exclusion of everything else. You will have to use reason here and make sure you are being safe. Conversely, once the mind has been trained to focus, it will yield a power that is unmatched.

Let me ask you a question here, do you finish what you start? It is of vital importance that we finish everything we start. It does not matter how big or small, once we start something we must see it through to the end. It also does not matter if the thing we started is important or not. The level of importance is not relevant; what is important, however, is that we finish it. We must become conscious of our responsibility to be responsible. Imagine the set back if Thomas Edison had given up on the light bulb on his 999th effort; it was the 1000th that yielded success.

Our children came to us, and we must let them grow into their own characters. Yet, we must continue raising them even if we are unsure of their age of maturity. If every person who had ever attempted a new thing quit before its completion, this world would still be in its primitive state. This is the science. When we start a thing and quit, the message to the subjective mind is that this is the norm; in other words, this is what I do. Thus, the more we quit on things, the more it will be our reality. By contrast, the opposite is also true; when we do what we say we will and complete it that also becomes our normal habit. That is when we should consciously proclaim this is the real me; I always complete what I start. To build a habit of following through on our commitments give us power. Each person must decide what he or she wants to reflect on in the golden years. Do you want your reflection to be on a life of regret, or one of accomplishments? The choice is ours; harness your power.

What We Know

"If you stop seeking your reality, it will stop seeking you"

Many are frustrated with their current status and their lives and wish they could extricate themselves from current situations. On the other hand, the world is in a constant makeover remembering that nothing can stay the same. Still, we have to make sure that there is enough people with the right mindset to help keep the balance. If we continue to let others make decisions for us, it will not be in our best interest.

What are the impacts of generations upon generations of people in a state of mental repose? We must take note that we now have people with no direction/s. The citizens of the world are now looking towards their government for help, but in order to keep the world from falling apart, we need thinkers. Ordinary people must step up and start thinking for self. We are the help we are waiting on; like we said, source can't do for us what it can only do through us.

For help in over-standing our latent power we, again, must look at nature. We find prevalent in nature energies of the male and female correspondence. There are even male and female plants, flowers, and trees and the female still bears the fruit. There must be a reuniting of this male and female energy within our minds. This is to restore natural balance. Every aspect of the human being consists of the male and female energies.

What's more, the objective mind represents the male energy and the subjective mind the female. What we know is that, traditionally, the female gives birth on the physical plane. Since our physical forms are but a reflection of the mental and spiritual plane, we see that we are talking about energy. Therefore, we must impregnate the female with the male. Now once we plant the correct seed, it grows and births the right thought-child. This child will be vibrating on the same frequency of the thing we want; the condition we seek in life. Furthermore, this is the cause that will manifest the circumstance/s you want on this physical plane. Don't forget that everything vibrates; even a rock is a mass of vibrating energy. We can create our own reality!

The only question that remains is, will you take responsibility for your life? Some no doubt will stay in the waters of conformity and be boiled to death like a frog. It is high time you realize that the kingdom of heaven you seek resides within. The illusion can't change the omnipotent source, but the source can change the illusion. We are the medium by which this can be done. Though, it will take some thinking on our part and that will lay our path. As we think so shall we live!

No one has seen the mind at any time, however, we have observed the brain. Once a person's heart stop beating or his or her breathing stops, we can resuscitate them within limits today. A person can be in a coma for a long time and wake up, but if the mind leaves, the person is pronounced brain dead. So here it is, the mind actuates the brain and uses it. Without the mind the brain is useless, and since the mind tells the brain what to do the body cannot function without it. Once the mind; the I; the spirit leaves the physical dies. Energy is never really destroyed, although it does sometimes change its state.

Why is a rock a rock? A rock is a rock because of its rate of vibration and arrangement of the molecules. That would be the same with a diamond. On the other hand, if we could change the rate at which a diamond vibrates to that of a piece of coal, what would happen? The molecules of that diamond would rearrange to their new vibrations, that of a piece of coal. Thus, instead of a diamond you would now have a piece of coal. The only difference in the outward physical appearance of a thing is the rate of vibration that produces a particular arrangement of its molecular structure. In the same way, if you change the molecular structure you change the vibration. Let us use thoughts to change the neurons in our brains.

When we learn to use purposeful thinking that is concentrated on a specific ideal, it will result in that ideal being realized with and in accordance to the appropriate action. If you recall, we said that success is not a destination but a journey. When we learn to enjoy the journey, we will get to many destinations and each one being better than the last. Have you realized yet that we are like a molecule of water in the ocean thinking that we are different and separate from the ocean? Yet, water is water. Albeit, the difference of me throwing a glass of water in your face and you being hit with a tsunami shows contrast. The difference to that analogy is that we have the ability to think. Therefore, we have the ability to tap into the source and bring forth the tsunami.

Mind Independent of Body

The mind can and does exist outside of the body! I don't have to research or look this up, this I know as fact. Maybe a story here can best relate the truth of the matter. By story I mean it in the sense of a true account of an incident in my life. One day in mid-1982 I was asleep on a summer morning. I was very young at that time, about 22 years old.

My first wife and I were semi living together. Semi living together; you might be asking what that is, but that is the best I could describe that situation. At that time, we weren't married but just girlfriend and boyfriend.

Anyhow, I was asleep but I woke up as I heard some voices coming from the living room. As I approached the living room I saw my then girlfriend putting on her pants, a pair of jeans. I then looked to the left and saw one of her brother's standing there talking to her. I was not in an entertaining frame of mind so I went back to the bedroom and sat on the bed. While sitting on the bed, I turned and looked over my right shoulder at the bed, and had to do a double-take. What I mean by that is that I looked, turned my head back to the front, and when I realized what I saw I quickly looked back. And, to my amazement, I was right the first time. I saw my body still lying in the bed; that caused me to snap back in instantly and I woke up.

I then quickly went to the living room where I saw my girlfriend and asked her where is her brother; she said he just left. I then asked her if she had just put her cloths on in the living room and she said yes. She then said, "I thought you were sleeping." I replied, "I thought so too." Then, I related the whole incident to her. Isn't the mind amazing? If only we knew how to use it better. I have been trying to find the user's manual ever since.

The Mind Knows

On another occasion I had a different kind of encounter. I know that the mind knows all things since our mind (the subconscious) is part of the universal mind, and this source knows all things. This would mean that we can also know what we want too, given that we can get our knowledge from the source. Regardless of our station in life, if we develop our mental capacity we can gain access.

The body is at present appearances trapped in the present. Conversely, the mind is able to travel at will. Spirit is omnipresent and cannot be trapped, caged, or captured in any way. The Universal mind of which we are a part of is everywhere; we can't go any place where it is not. It is all and in all. All we need to do is think of a place and the mind is there.

On this occasion I was meditating. As I recalled, I had just moved into a small blue house that was completely empty. There was no furniture, not even a bed to sleep on. I had recently gone through my second divorce. So I sat on the floor during the shadow hours meditating; I think it was on divine love. Deep into meditation, my son appeared to me. Now, at that time he was only not even four years old and was kind of chubby. But, in my meditation he was standing by a kitchen sink and was tall and not chubby at all. Today he is 16 going on 17 years old and taller than me. There is a part that I left out because I don't want to influence his thinking but just observe the outcome. Given recognition, the mind can do the most amazing things. There were other experiences, but those I will keep to myself for now.

Where is the Help?

"If you accept your present reality, it will also accept you"

N ever ever accept your present condition in life, no matter what it may be. Have you ever noticed after moving into a nice neighborhood, after some time as we know it, sometimes the place seems to start falling apart? Yes. it was a so called nice place at first, so what happened? Those concerned started to say, "It is nice here, just leave it the way it is." But you forgot I said before, the only constant is change. Thus, since there was no more additional work done to the place because it was just fine, what happened? It fell apart little by little, and one day it appeared that you just woke up to a rundown neighborhood.

It is the same way with humans, the body and mind has to be cultivated at all times. Our circumstances we must strive to forever improve. The fool goes backward and stays in a reclining state. Our minds will give to us whatever we ask of it, big or small. Did you get that? This is a revelation I had to learn the hard way. Some people go through life thinking they have to beg others to help them make it through a reality manifested by the self; they are constantly trying to find a source outside of self for help. The truth of the matter is that the source of our help is within. When we go inside (of self), we will attract the right people to us. By default, these people will help even without our knowledge.

When we think the wrong thoughts, we will repel our help and attract negative people to us; negative in the sense that they will be contrary to what we currently need. On the other hand, when we are thinking right, we become a magnet and people say we are lucky. It is not luck; it is a science. Our minds can give us everything we want. What is your truth? The truth shall indeed make us free.

I have been to the school of business and one thing I can say for sure is that when a person is ready to do business he or she most know the investment needed, the breakeven point, and profit margin in a nutshell. In other words, people don't go into business guessing if they are to have a chance at succeeding; they must know certain truths. Find out the truth about you, and be honest. What is the reality that you strive in really like? Live the truth and let it be your religion. Know that the real you are spirit, and therefore, the essence of perfection. When you say no one is perfect that includes you consciously and subconsciously. Thus, you open up yourself for imperfect things to happen; we are spirit and spirit is perfect. That is, until you decide that you are not.

You hold the key to life in your head; you hold the key to succeed or fail. The key will be used on purpose or by chance, all the same your condition is not by chance. The law is exact. The moment you decide you consciously choose your faith. Then, your key opens the book and all you have to do is flip the page/s. And, as you read the book, you may rewrite the words to reflect the new author's life. Live your life on demand, and be your best self; the choice is yours.

Inspiration 16

The Concept of One

"Before we can control conditions, we must control ourselves; if you do not conquer self, you will be conquered by self"

There are many who regard Adam Smith as the father of capitalism. Smith believed that the illusion of individualism should be recognized as such; in that, people should toil with the sole intention of bettering oneself alone. We agree that we should utilize our gift of thinking to improve ourselves because, as previously stated, everything and a person are intended to grow. We should grow to our fullest potential. If we are not growing, we are declining. Change must and will occur. Nevertheless, we are gathering information to the betterment of all.

One of the areas where we differ from Adam Smith's concept of capitalism is when he implied that an unknown force will take care of society as a whole, and the impression is, he was talking about those less fortunate. Or, in different words, those who have not yet discovered the workings of the mind will be looked after by forces unknown. If that was truly the case, we will not have people starving all over this planet. Thus, we feel differently; we should use this knowledge to bring us wealth in all its forms, such as health, love, friends, and money. But, the ideal we manifest to bring us monetary wealth should be an idea whose manifestation will better the conditions of the many. With great reward comes great responsibility is the saying of the day. To receive much the same must be given, and the more help we render to others, the bigger the reward.

If we accept that we came from one source, then we must realize that we look in a large mirror every day to see many views and aspects of the self; each reflection of self means getting a different experience, and therefore, building its own characteristics. This would be like the water in the lake; the water in the river; the water in the swamp; the water in the form of ice; and the water that is boiled and turned into a gas. Yet, all this liquid, solid, and gas is still water and could be nothing else but water. The human body starts off as one cell and as a grown person have thousands of cells within one body. Still, the body is one. But, if the cells that make up a certain organ within that body go out of tune with the body and become a renegade, the whole body suffers.

The aforementioned in and of itself is a great revelation for the thinking man or woman. We give you the concept of one. That is the law. If a few go off and become renegades and betray the oneness of the human race, the whole will suffer the consequences of the few. We should live the good life, but not at the expense of others, but to their betterment. When we look at selfish people, we find that they have a scarcity mentality. Yet, there is no scarcity in nature, all we find is abundance. There is enough for all to have and live the good life here. This is so, even more, when we use our mental capacity to create a way for the masses to strive. Then, the abundance becomes apparent to us, individually. What seems to be more the case is that this gift of thought is being used to make weapons of mass destruction instead; this is because of the promotion of fear.

Our thinking process can be used to create things that would only benefit a few and be lucrative. However, based on this law, it is certain that any apparent success will not be sustained long term. All one has to do is look at history and see that those things that were selfish, relative to a person or race, declines. And, no one country stays in power forever. This is so because while the one country may be helping other less accomplished ones, many other countries are neglected. This does not fulfill the law of one. We can't just help those who fit our personal agendas.

Many have tried and still try today to work around this law to no ends. It may seem to you that some are succeeding at breaking this law. Nevertheless, our lifetime is but a flash-in-the-pan and in the longer- now they must fail; the law is immutable. If we somehow found a way to prolong an unnatural way of life that benefitted the few, that country or system will eventually be in a state of confusion just like a diseased body. Just take a good look at history and/or life today.

A Physical Experience

"The great achiever that lay asleep in your holly temple
(brain) is your mind"

At times I have heard people say they are having, or has had a spiritual experience. That is a statement I tend to ponder on every time I hear it. I do so because I know that we are spiritual beings and our predominant experience should be spiritual in nature. Accordingly, we are here on this planet having a physical experience. To think otherwise would mean that you are permanently living in a dream state without knowing that you are dreaming. What I mean by that is this, in our day-to-day interaction we are really in a dream state. When we go off to be (to be, as in being, in our true spiritual state while sleeping in the shadow hours) and start so-called dreaming, that state I think is more real to our nature than the physical experiences we live every day. We have now come to call the vehicle the passenger and the passenger the vehicle. Know that our bodies are merely our vehicles that we use to move around on this physical plane. The real you, me, us, the I is a spirit and the passenger.

When a person losses a limb from an accident it is said that he or she still feels as though the body part is still there. Why is that? Think about it. The physical body part is gone but the feeling of having the part is still present. This is because the germ that grows to form the body is grown around the spiritual form we take on here. So, the physical outward appearance is but a reflection of what the spiritual wants to individualize here. The body doesn't form and then the spirit fills it, it is the other way around. Therefore, life exists as what we consider a child before the actual physical form starts to take actual form. This would mean that a being has entered its mother's womb even before physical conception, and just maybe, as with all else, it starts with the meeting of the minds.

Life, The Great Spirit, God as we would have it is really the All and is seeking experience and self-expression. As a result, it is written that we may know that this expression (God) is everywhere. This energy, spirit is everywhere and in all, it is ALL. You can't take from it or add to it as it is all conclusive and inclusive. It is all and all is in us; therefore, I am you and you are me. Yet, we are separate in nature as we individualized ourselves to experience this school. However, since we are part of this great force we are the same in kind and likeness to it. Thus, it is written that we are in the image of God (ALL). Learn to think beyond the physical. Is the water in the glass different than the water in the ocean? No, the only difference is in that of degree.

We must have faith in our mental abilities. We created this physical world around us; consequently, it would hold true that we can control it even as we control our own bodies. After all, collectively, we are the ones seeking all experience of the physical; so, we can choose what we wish to experience here. For those who don't know, there is a science referred to as Kirlian photography that shows what is unseen by the natural eyes. Named after its parent, Semyon Davidovich Kirlian a Russian inventor, Kirlian photography captures the life force emanating from all living things. This is virtually a glimpse of the real you. However, once the vehicle becomes irreparable the passenger leaves.

This physical experience is but a flash-in-the-pan. Consider the many souls in the physical who have experience the heat of the sun and behold it through physical eyes since this school began. Yet, the sun a ball of energy lives on for thousands of years. Still, that too is just a reflection of the source seeking expression within its self. Nonetheless, if that sun was to become extinguished, all life on earth will cease to exist. The sun in the sky is indeed our sustainer.

The Illusion

When we leave this physical body we are still able to think. When I traveled outside my body in 1982, I was still able to think as usual. If we needed the brain for this function, why was that possible? The brain is the control center from which the mind, spiritual intelligence, commands. The control center, known as the central nervous system, is the point from which all bodily functions are carried out. But, the brain again is not the mind. Mind is spirit. The brain is what mind uses to control the body. The source of this spiritual intelligence can be likened unto what is considered static energy until placed into motion by its creation looking for individualized experience.

You may be asking yourself, is any of this real? Are the lives we live real or an illusion? I would reply by asking you, real compared to what? Your life is real as much as you are a real living spiritual entity! We are real. We have feelings, which in reality is feeling as in singular, the only physical sense. And, we have an inner knowing that there is more than what we can physically see. We are life itself seeking to be.

However, the illusion is this, most of us tend to think that what we see on the outside is the real us. But we should not look at the hologram as real nor seek our answers from it. The hologram is real only to the extent that we make it real. When we seek answers from an illusion and build on it, we, in fact, support the lie that takes us further from the truth. We start believing in and depending on the outer creation instead of the inner creator. This is the spirit of truth!

When we look in the mirror at what we believe to be self, we only see the tip of the iceberg or pyramid. When we look at a pyramid what we see is an illusion of what a pyramid really is. There is just as much buried that hides its true appearance, and so much more within the pyramid. You must enter the pyramid to find its true treasures and the secret of the pyramid treasures is found within. Thus, to find truth we must look to the point of origin of the hologram. Still we must know the rules and nature of the reality we physically exist in. The journey here is a 50-50 one and but a flash-in-the- pan of existence.

The Living Mind

"Mr. and Mrs. Potter start molding your life"

Man and mind are one, without mind there is no man and without man there is no known intelligent representation on mind. When the term, man is used, it is to represent intelligent biological life on and off our spaceship called earth. Mind-spirit is the origin of the hologram we refer to as reality. As well, every living thing in existence (animated and unanimated) is a representation of The All as mind and its expression respectively in different vibrational modes. Yet, emotion in man which is the motion of energy is what causes the physical action. Mind is the point of origin. Man in his core existence is spirit.

The mind cannot be caged, locked in a vault, or be destroyed. Consequently, the essence of man is life itself, and that life cannot be destroyed. This would mean that life can only be life. Nothing is truly destroyed but is just changed in form. Let's take a look at water again. If water is frozen into a solid, when we speed up its molecules by using heat it is changed into a liquid and then into a vapor. The vapor then assimilates into the atmosphere; we are then unable to see it, yet it still exists.

Mind can destroy or it can create form, it is the true cause behind every action that caused the reaction. Thus, the effect is the result of mind in action. Know that mind in action is thought. Therefore, critical thinking is a must if we are to create a reality conducive to our true nature. But, we must first have that inner knowing from our higher-self, we must feel it. When we build our thoughts from this inner knowing, it leads to right thinking. We consequently can create a hell or a heaven for ourselves.

We give up this power to control our lives when we seek help from the outside. We then place ourselves at the mercy of unconscious mental programming and other people's ideas for us. And, since most other people think as individuals, you as one, set yourself up as part of the rat-race because the part they will give you to play is to further their illusion of individual self. Not your individualized self, theirs!

The God you are looking for can only be found within. You have a direct line to this reality through your objective, subjective, and sympathetic mind. This is your direct connection to the mental reservoir and the All that you refer to as God.

Does Man Create or God?

Man and what is framed God are the same, that means in kind and quality. Without the source, there will be non in existence as all life receives life from this life force or source. All of our ancient writings seem to agree on this fact which makes us part of The All. We even find within the human body all that is known physically to exist in support of life. The outer world and universe reflects our inner; we have an inner-verse that projects our reality.

There is no difference in a small part from the whole and, thus, this is the creativity in man. Man is as God. The only difference in this observation is to the degree to which we are. However, you can't be The All but can be one with all. I am happy to be part of all which is the source of my life. In the physical dimension man makes things from things that are already in existence, but all things created from nothingness is created of the source. As a matter of fact, the state of nothingness was also a necessary creation from which all things had to emanate.

For instance, if you walked into a classroom to teach mathematics and the blackboard was full of writings, the board will have to be erased before you can write the new formulas on it. Thus, you would have created a state of nothingness from where you can build new thoughts. In the same way, if you entered this classroom with preconceived notions on what the curriculum contains and how it should be taught, you may find it hard to learn. You must empty your cup before you walk in, or there will be no room for learning. Of course, this example is limited relative to, for lack of a better wording, divine creation.

Inspiration 19

Spiritual Activity

"Where there is Imagination and Faith, we find great
Achievements"

Now, in retrospect, we declared that we have an objective mind which is relative to our subjective mind that is our connection to the mental reservoir. This mental reservoir is sometimes referred to as Source, the Godhead, the Universal Mind, and so many other names on this planet. It is part of the ALL. This all knowing power is spirit. Because this all knowing power is spirit and the thought of ALL, it would hold true that since collective mind produce thought, then, it is of the ALL. Thus, thought is essentially sprit. And, everything must be created in the spiritual world before it can take form in the physical. Note that the brain (our bio-computer) is not the mind, but is actuated by the mind; and, mind as spirit is creative force.

I do not know what your beliefs are. Still, when we consider the heaven and the earth and all that is within it and how each creation is perfectly in support of each other, we must ask, what is the intelligence that can accomplish this? It is the same intelligence that we have access to as thought, if we would but put ourselves in tune with this force. We become the captain of our ships. We are in all and all is in us; when we become aware of this we must set out to claim our birthright.

This is what I know:

Spirituality

Most people, if you ask them, "Who are you? Tell me a little about yourselves!" They will start by describing their personalities, some of their likes and dislikes, and their physical characteristics. With the implication that this is who they are, when in fact, the first is the way you act and react founded on your life experiences. The second is a regiment of acceptations and rejections, based on one's perception. And, the third is her/his cultural and personal uniqueness of matter.

Matter, this is an interesting word. What exactly is matter? All matter is made up of the same substance, and when looked at closer it is not that unique at all, but unto itself. Matter can appear to be a solid, liquid, or of gas. The right microscope would reveal that all known things on earth are of the same substance. This is true, whether they are plants, rocks to include gems, water, and minerals, animals, or Homo sapiens. They all consist of **atoms** which are made up of protons, neutrons, and electrons that are further broken down to quarks, of which, scientists have now found to be made of pure **energy**. So, matter is, in fact, pure energy. With that being the case, this would make us not physical but spiritual beings, with powers unknown to most. The only difference, in the outer shape and appearance of things to include Homo sapiens, would be a result of the arrangements of the atoms. Also, the speed at which this energy is vibrating becomes a major factor.

We are cosmic beings, and are smaller parts of the cosmos, existing in The All as minuet parts of The All; we are to The All as atoms are to us. Atoms are so small that they are unperceivable by our naked eyes. Yet, they are us! They (atoms) make up our inner-verse; a *concept* of having our own universe within us. While, in turn, we help make up the universe/s.

Psychologists have long been exploring the human mind, in reality, they are trying to understand deity. The mind is the universal consciousness that brought into existence the universes with all their animated and seemingly inanimate things. There is but one mind, and we all tap into this great conscious entity. We are but a thought in a world of illusions seeking our independent experiences. Yet, we are one! And, as water seeks to find itself, we search for our true selves; mind, body, and soul are our trinity. If you take a glass of water from the ocean, is it still water? So, why are you trying to be independent of source? We are All but One in All!

Let us take a look at the word psychology. According to the Online Etymology Dictionary, Noah Webster's dictionary first published 1828: psyche: 1647, "animating spirit," from L. Psyche, from Gk. psykhe, "the soul, mind, spirit, breath, Life, the invisible animation principle or entity which occupies and directs the physical body" (personified as Psykhe, the lover of Eros), akin to psykhein "to blow, cool," from PIE base *bhes- "to blow" (cf. Skt. Bhas-). The word had extensive sense development in Platonic philosophy and Jewish-infl. theological writing of St. Paul. In Eng., psychological sense is from 1910.

Psychology: 1653, "study of the soul," probably coined mid-16c., in Germany by Melanchthon as Mod. L. psychologia, from Gk. psykhe- "breath, spirit, soul" (see *psyche*) + logia "study of." Meaning "study of the mind" first recorded 1748, from G. Wolff's Psychologia empirica (1732); main modern behavioral sense is from 1895.

Religion has nothing to do with spirituality. Some people get confused when talking about religion and spirituality; they think religion and spirituality are one and the same. Religion instead, is a systematic approach at controlling one's thought process and emotions, which in turn, controls her/his actions. Spirituality, on the other hand, is the expression of mind, in man's approach to discovering his/her higher self by exploring his/her inner-verse. By coming in contact with his/her higher self, he/she can now make the connection with the universal All-knowing mental reservoir, which is of The All. The All is being referred to as God in Christian religions; or, Deity in each respective religion. This process is sometimes called self-realization, and it is said a person's third eye is open, or the All-Seeing-Eye which interchangeably is used when also speaking of The All Consciousness.

We are to become consciously aware of our spiritual unity with The All. Know that we have a direct connection. I am not talking about religion here. Hear me clearly! We have to use a systematic approach to get back in tune first with ourselves, then with Mother Nature and the Universal Mind. Realize that divine truth is our birthright.

In the end, we will all revert to our original form which is the spirit form. It is the next step. The day we entered into physical form we progressively entered a state of spiritual forgetfulness. Some of us are waking up to this realization by trying to find our way back home while yet in the physical. The adage, "you must be born again of spirit and of truth" is really saying we must re-emerge into source being born into the spiritual realm from whence we came knowing all truths. We must reconnect with that from whence we came and yet exist in. Does not water return to its source and like attract like? The connection was and is always there, all one has to do is look.

Closing Remarks

Know this: whether or not we play an active role in changing our lives, it will change. The only difference will be if we have a deciding factor in that change. The only constant is change. So, change must and will come. I suggest to you that we stop trying to make a living and learn how to designing our individual life. I have rewritten my life in the process of writing this book; I changed my now. Now it is your turn to rewrite your life.

So too, we must become balanced beings. This means that we need to develop the male and female energies within us. I am saying that males must have a fifty-fifty balance as with the females. To be clear, I am talking about emotional, mental, and spiritual stability. This should be done before we seek a mate. If we do not balance ourselves before seeking a relationship with the opposite sex, the relationship will be in turmoil.

This is so because the male will be feeding on his mate's energies and the female on her mate's. Eventually, such a relationship will end. Once we have our own balance, we need not feed on others and can now truly help each other. Thus, we must present a whole self; we owe it to our potential partners and ourselves. Learn to relate to self; for, how can we relate to a mate if we cannot even relate to the self?

Finally, look within, there is no God but he/she that dwells in me and I in you; there is a doorway to you inside of me. Therefore, be still in meditation and know that I am....

Let us raise the vibration on this planet together that we may preserve it for our future generations.

THINK, THINK, THINK...

Thank you for reading this book

Your thoughts hold the answers to a better you, and as such, your mind is the gateway to a better life!

Inspiration Corner
Notes

Thank you for reading this book

Aspire to be greater than you are
today…

About the Author

A retired Marine and graduate from the School of Business, Anthony Williams, set out to raise the bar for personal transformation. He has led and inspired Marines to transform their lives during his 20-year run in the Marine Corps. Now, he has taken that same leadership to the next level of inspiring the world to a higher consciousness.

Deeply committed to contributing, Anthony Williams set his sights on making a difference with "Inspiration Corner". In it, he gives us the mechanics of inner-change because as he so astutely stated, "when we can change our mental state, we would have changed our future." Anthony returned to school and obtained his four year business degree after retiring from the Marine Corps. This was to show his children that it is never too late to achieve one's goals.

Anthony Williams has been a student of this information for over 35 years. He has studied the exoteric and esoteric of life changing knowledge while a member of certain societies. And, while he teaches from these platforms, no oaths have been broken. We now have the opportunity to learn from Anthony's knowledge how civilians transform into Marines, along with his 35-year plus research in this field (personal Power).

Thank you for reading this book

www.ingramcontent.com/pod-product-compliance
Lightning Source LLC
Chambersburg PA
CBHW071638050426
42443CB00026B/710